all our
own work

thank
you

HOW TO
BE A
MOTORIST

Cars To Suit All Figures

HOW TO
BE A
MOTORIST

By

HEATH ROBINSON
and
K.R.G. BROWNE

Learning to steer

This edition first published in 2015 by the
Bodleian Library
Broad Street
Oxford OX1 3BG

www.bodleianshop.co.uk

ISBN: 978 1 85124 434 8

First published in 1939 by Hutchinson & Co. Ltd.

Cover design by Dot Little at the Bodleian Library
Designed and typeset by Roderick Teasdale in 11.5pt on 11.5pt
Tw Cen MT Light

Printed and bound on 90gsm munken cream by
TJ International Ltd., Padstow, Cornwall

British Library Catalogue in Publishing Data
A CIP record of this publication is available from the British Library

The Latest

Cop-Comfort

CONTENTS

Alpine Difficulties

DEDICATION

This handy, decorative, valuable, and uncostly volume, on which so much loving care and ink has been expended by the compilers, is dedicated in admiring sympathy (on the artist's part) and sympathetic admiration (on the author's) to that badgered but unconquerable little creature, the British Motorist, or Fate's football.

In England nowadays it is practically impossible to be both law-abiding and a car-owner; try as the latter may to keep abreast of the regulations, new ones pop up at the rate of six a week to confound and abash him. His not to reason why; his not even to make reply when browbeaten by a beak for committing one of the 11,437 major crimes or one of the 27,812 minor offences in the motoring calendar; his but to bow the head and cough up the sum demanded.

In view of the fact that he is nearly always the goat, and regarded by the Treasury as an unfailing fount of gold, it says much for the British Motorist's skill, nerve, and sense of direction that he so seldom gets quodded for more than three years at a stretch or fined more than £50 at one go. And if this little book proves in any way helpful to him in his efforts to stay out of gaol and hang on to his savings, nobody will be gladder than us (or more glad than we, if you prefer it).

That will be all—and quite enough, too, in our opinion.

Wayside Shave

The Introduction

INTRODUCTION

As one trudges along Life's highway, humming an old Andalusian air and in momently peril of annihilation by mechanically propelled vehicles bearing coals to Newcastle, stockbrokers to Brighton, or football addicts to Cup Finals, one is apt to forget that motoring, as a pastime for the masses, has yet to celebrate its half-century.

Yet so, as a glance at the archives will bear witness, it is. The automobile (a'to-mo-bil, *n.* Gr. *auto,* self) if not exactly in its infancy, is still some way from its second childhood. As late as the closing days of the Victorian era, when the bustle was a common object of the countryside and wireless Talks on Economics were mercifully hidden in the future, the transport problem was a constant worry to the citizen who was scared of horses, allergic to trains, and ill at ease on penny-farthing bicycles. He could walk, or he could stay at home, but there was no middle course. And then somebody, killing time between meals or trying to take his mind off the Repeal of the Corn Laws, up and invented the motor-car; and—bing!—life took on a new aspect for high and low alike.

In its young days, of course, motoring was no hobby for the aged and infirm, or for those who shrank from publicity. Like the mind of a Cabinet Minister—or a hen under the influence of vodka—the early motor-car moved in such mysterious ways that it was often hard to

Mr. Heath Robinson's

say if it were coming, going, or just oscillating slightly. Viewed with grave suspicion by the Law and with amused contempt by the general public, the pioneer motorist needed the hide of a rhinoceros, the optimism of a spaniel pup, and the physical endurance of a female hockey player; also a joke-proof constitution, a cap with ear-flaps, some stout walking-boots, and a good deal of spare cash.

In those days, in fact, one had to be pretty tough to own and/or drive a car. Though the late-Victorian automobile could always be trusted to stop, it could not always—or even often—be relied on to start; while its tendency, when flustered, to dissolve into its component parts was a perpetual annoyance to its occupants. Moreover, on the rare occasions when,

AUXILIARY POWER

Home-made "Carmactor"

Extra Streamline

with the help of St. Christopher and a following wind, it travelled more than a mile without blowing up or falling apart, a summons for driving to the danger of the public was generally the result.

Like the first umbrella, the first warthog, and the first tapioca pudding, the first motor-car was regarded by the said public as a rather laboured joke. To the simple peasantry, as it leaned on gates and hurled rude jests and occasional wurzels at the weird machines that staggered past, each preceded by a standard-bearer with a crimson banner (to warn the totally deaf of the

The Correspondence Course

approach of Juggernaut), it seemed unlikely that these bizarre contraptions could ever earn their keep. As a rival to the long-established and justly popular horse, the horseless carriage was hardly anybody's fancy.

Well, things are different now, as will be apparent to anybody who cares to loiter in the middle of Hammersmith Broadway during the evening rush-hour. Little by little, horseless carriages have improved and developed until nowadays they are all over the place, and people who have never owned or driven one are considered slightly odd; while the horse, broadly speaking, now exists only by courtesy of those who need something larger than a greyhound to put their shirts on. It would take too long to detail the various steps whereby this change has come about, but we trust the reader will accept the evidence of his own eyes—if neither Mr. Heath Robinson's word nor mine is good enough for him—that it *has* done so.

For good or ill, in other words, the motor-car has come to stay. Realizing this—for little escapes our

For Rapid Reversing—Backwards Streamline

Calculating the Horse-Power

notice, palsied dotards though we may appear to the casual observer—Mr. Heath Robinson and I have laboured night and day (approximately four of each, to be exact) to produce this little book for the guidance of those about to join the motoring classes for the first time. Although cars are more numerous in kids in many English households, there are still some people who have never yet set foot to clutch or scared the pants off a pedestrian, but every year a number of these pull up their socks and take the plunge at the insistence of their wives or other relatives who hold that donkey-drawn governess-carts are hopelessly *vieux jeu* today.

Though it is chiefly for such beginners that this work has been devised, the experienced road-hog who needs something to read in traffic-blocks will find it pretty instructive, too. Apart from Mr. Heath Robinson and myself, nobody knows *everything* about motoring; indeed, many motorists now at large know practically

INTRODUCTION

of a Sports Car

nothing, if one may judge by their behaviour on the road. Everybody, in short, who is ever likely to drive, be driven in, or get run over by a mechanically propelled vehicle will find something of interest in the following pages, in which we have torn aside the veil that shrouds the workings of a motor-car from the layman's eye, and laid bare the many pitfalls awaiting the free-born Englishman who has the confounded impudence (from the point of view of the policeman, the pedestrian and the cyclist) to be a motorist.

As to our qualifications for this task, it should suffice to say that Mr. Heath Robinson, at the wheel of his home-made carmactor (which can be used as a caravan, a mangle or a tractor, as desired), is a familiar and respected figure on several suburban by-roads, while I have had my present car—"Old Tinribs", as the neighbours call it laughingly—ever since it was a tiny motor-scooter.

So there it is. And if, after this book has been in circulation for a month or two, we do not receive a couple of knighthoods, or at the very least a brace of pheasants, for our services to the cause of Road Safety, we shall feel—to put it bluntly—that justice has not been done.

Interesting Ceremony at the End of the Course

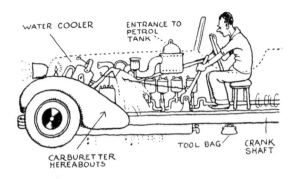

*Section Through Mr. K.R.G. Browne's New Sports Car,
showing Drive and Water-Cooling System*

HOW A CAR WORKS

To qualify as a seasoned motorist of the sort that reckons his mileage in millions and has more or less atrophied legs, it is obviously necessary to acquire a rough working knowledge of What Makes The Wheels Go Round. This is easy enough, of course, for the mechanically minded—those enviable souls who have only to glance swiftly at a piece of machinery to know exactly why the gimble-valves oscillate transversely with the sump-rod, and what happens when the inward movement of the torque-bracket coincides with the down-thrust of the exhaust-cam.

To such fortunates the interior economy of a motor-car is as an open book, but to the mutton-headed majority it is as incomprehensible as the regulations

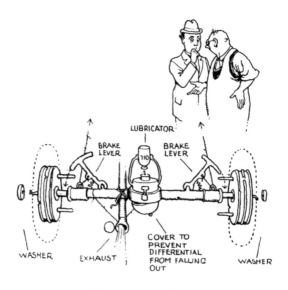

A Typical Back Axle Unit

governing the sale of cooked provisions on Early Closing Days. One may safely say, indeed, that a charge of swanshot fired at random in any direction could hardly fail to hit somebody who could not distinguish a valve-spring from a vasculum, and who would not recognize a gudgeon-pin if it were handed to him on a salver, and it is for the benefit of such that this chapter has been devised. Though the modern motor-car is so nearly foolproof that the veriest cretin can make it start and stop, a slight knowledge of what goes on under the bonnet is essential to the self-respecting motorist.

Hence the following revelations, which are aimed at the novice rather than at the expert. (The latter, in fact, has our permission to skip the next few pages —though we would ask him not to cut them out and use them to fan soup, etc., as such practices detract from the second-hand value of the book.)

As is fairly well known by this time, the motive power of the modern automobile is petrol (obtainable from wayside pumps or in two-gallon tins). The peculiar property of this fluid—which can also be used to erase tripe-stains from Court breeches—is that when ignited it explodes; and it was while pondering this idiosyncrasy one wet Sunday afternoon that somebody whose name escapes me, exclaimed "Eureka!" and invented the internal-combustion engine.

Briefly, the latter is so designed that when petrol is fed into it and vaporized by a simple dingus called a "carburettor", and then set alight by a thing known as a "sparking-plug", a series of jolly little explosions takes place and continues to do so until the petrol runs out or the clarion summons of the dinner-gong impels somebody to switch off the ignition.

How to Break Records in Comfort
Section Through the "Miami Belle"

(In very large and costly cars, such as those in which financiers and film stars visit their aged parents in the almshouse, this operation creates so little noise that it is hard to believe that it is actually occurring. But the motorist who likes to be certain about these things can always reassure himself by placing an ear close to the exit end of the exhaust-pipe—which will be found projecting from the stern of the vehicle—when he will hear a gentle puttering sound and stand a good chance of being overcome by carbon monoxide.)

All right so far? Very well, then. By an ingenious device which I have neither the time nor the inclination (nor, to be quite frank, the knowledge) to explain here, the force of these explosions is directed against a bevy or gaggle of small cylindrical objects, resembling solid metal jampots and known to the intelligentsia as "pistons". Startled by this onslaught—as who wouldn't be?—the pistons go hurriedly up and down, thus imparting a brisk rotary movement to what is wittily termed the "crank-shaft". And *that*, of course, makes the wheels go round.

But only the *back* wheels, mark you, exhaustive experiments over a period of years having proved that if these can be dragooned into revolving, the front wheels have no choice but to do likewise. Now and again, as one goes inquiringly about the world, one comes upon a car whose engine prefers to operate the *front* wheels, leaving the back ones to follow as best they may, but the drawback to this dodge, it seems to

Section Through Mr. Heath Robinson's 2-Cyl. 4-Seater Saloon

A Severe Test

me, is that if one forgets to remove the hand-brake (as the best of us are apt to do occasionally in the rush and bustle of life), the car is liable to come in half, causing roars of laughter.

Mention of brakes reminds me that these are almost as important a feature of the motor-car as its engine, about which Mr. Heath Robinson and myself have no further information to offer, having none in stock. True, without the engine there would be no need for brakes, but, on the other hand, without brakes it would be highly impolitic to use the engine. (This is known as Rambottle's Law, or the Compensation of Averages, and may be set to music and sung in public without fee.)

for Front Axle Springs

Like potatoes, gumboots and Society matrons, internal-combustion engines come in a variety of sizes. For purposes of comparison, the propelling ability of each engine is reckoned in terms of "horse-power", on the broad principle that ten horses can pull an Alderman's family from Walthamstow to Worthing in twice the time required by twenty horses to do the same job. No special breed of horse is recommended by the authorities for these calculations, but it is obviously inadvisable to mix them, since a team of, say, ten pure-bred Arab stallions will inevitably give better results than one comprising four cabhorses, three Percherons, two selling-platers and a Shetland pony.

HOW TO BE A MOTORIST

In the early days of the motor industry, two (2) brakes—one for each rear wheel—were considered ample, as the typical car of that period needed little encouragement to stop. Nowadays, however, a car with fewer than four—two forrard, two aft—is regarded as hopelessly *démodé* and seldom ridden in by anybody who can afford not to. This development has made life a good deal rosier for motorists who like to stop in a hurry on meeting a herd of oxen at a blind corner or encountering an unforeseen Alp in the dark.

"Yes, yes", the intelligent but testy reader may interject at this point, if he/she has survived so long, "so much is apparent to the crassest numbskull! But what of the electricity without which—unless Dame Rumour lies—no motor-car, however lavishly endowed with brakes, can function as advertised? Whence comes this vital spark, and how?"

Well, Sir or Madam, one of the most engaging characteristics of the modern automobile is that it manufactures its own electricity as it bowls along, now swerving deftly to avoid a cyclist, now scaring a deaf pedestrian practically out of his pants, and now inflicting a nervous breakdown upon a truant hen. This feat (impossible, incidentally, to the average Member of Parliament or trainer of racing newts) it accomplishes with the help of a "dynamo", which is roughly what its name implies and may be found, after considerable search, in a remote sitting-out place in the chassis, as the basement of the car is called in deference to the French.

The current thus cleverly generated explodes the petrol as and when required. Nay, more—it enables the motorist to dazzle all comers with a brace of powerful headlights (a great improvement on the candle-lamps behind which his predecessors crept spasmodically to Brighton and back, with luck), to rend the very heavens with peremptory blasts of his horn, and even, if he has the necessary flex and attachment, to operate a small vacuum-cleaner or electric razor while the car is actually in motion. More than that, I feel, one would scarcely dare to ask.

From the foregoing broad survey of the subject, it should be pretty clear to all that the modern car's ability to go places is due to no haphazard combination of circumstances, but to a carefully thought-out plan. Every nut, bolt, gadget and doohickus on the vehicle fulfils a definite purpose, and woe betide the novice motorist who removes, say, the sparking-plugs because their shape offends his eye!

*Sectional View of Car Showing Efficacy of Auxiliary
Flat-Iron Brakes*

But the beginner, when he signs his will, puts out the cat, commends himself to the care of Providence and takes the road for the first time, need not worry unduly about the complex mechanical processes occurring before, beneath and behind him. Provided he keeps to the left and puts in a little petrol now and then, his car will bear him hither and yon until he gets into arrears with his deferred payments and has to give it back.

For his further enlightenment, however, there is appended an explanatory diagram of a typical modem chassis, showing the approximate whereabouts of nearly everything mentioned in this chapter. As this particular chassis has been standing in an open field for several months, while its lamps, carburettor, sparking-plugs and dynamo were sold some time ago in aid of charity, it is not, perhaps, in the best of condition. It has

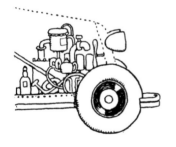

*For the
Constant
Lubrication
of the
Back Axle*

Testing a New Type of Steering Gear

also, in the course of time, acquired certain accessories, not commonly regarded as standard, which Mr. Heath Robinson—a stickler for detail and an ardent Nature-lover—has insisted on putting in.

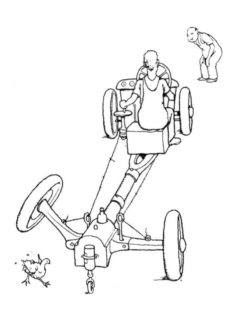

The New Rear Wheel Lift for Avoiding Obstacles

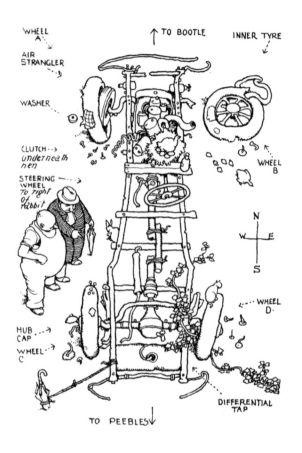

Explanatory Diagram of a Typical Modern Chassis

Still, as it is the only specimen available for demonstration purposes, we can only ask our great, bat-headed public to make allowances, take the rough with the smooth, accept the simple gift in the spirit in which it is offered, and oblige.

The Car Is Liable To Come In Half

Round Cars for Round People

HOW TO CHOOSE A CAR

It goes without saying—but it shall be said, all the same, because this chapter must be filled somehow, and every little helps—that a motor-car should be chosen pretty carefully, much as one chooses a cigar or a companion for a walking tour, rather than haphazardly and on the impulse of the moment, as one chooses a pair of sock-suspenders or a wife. To rush into the nearest sale-room, close the eyes, turn round three times, point at random and exclaim, "I'll have that one!" is to invite big trouble in the future.

Before taking the initial step, in other words, the embryo motorist must give careful thought to such considerations as (a) his size and shape, (b) the views of his wife and family, and (c) the temperament and general outlook on life of his bank manager; and of these (c) is probably the most important. Thanks to the well-known and justly popular Instalment System, cars can be obtained nowadays on Terms so Easy that the bulk of the expense falls on the original purchaser's grandchildren, but it should be remembered that payment *too* long deferred maketh the payee's heart sick.

The wise beginner, therefore, will buy a car he can afford, rather than one that he can maintain only by selling his furniture, sending his wife out to work, and subsisting on odd crusts begged from door to door. And before reaching for his cheque-book and giving the decisive nod that will enable the salesman to enjoy an extra egg with his tea, he must obviously decide what *type* of car he wants.

For persons of mature years and untough constitution, the closed or saloon car is clearly the most suitable, as it keeps the elements out and its inmates dry during the fiercest English summer. The young and hardy,

Being Measured for a New Car

on the other hand, tend to prefer a roofless model of the sort that combines the minimum of comfort with the maximum of noise, and so gives the impression of being far quicker than it actually is. And for the grossly rich, of course, a vast and gleaming limousine, with detachable chauffeur and a horn like the Last Trump, is the only possible choice.

This, however, is a point on which every intending car-owner must obey the dictates of his own heart, with a little assistance from those of his wife's. In the same way, he must wrestle with himself in the night-watches until he can decide whether he wants a brand-new vehicle, hot from the factory and glittering like mad, or a second-hand article that has seen a bit of life. A second-hand car is usually cheaper than a newly hatched one of the same species, but its tendency to come unstuck somewhere is proportionately greater.

But whatever type of horseless carriage he finally selects, the novice motorist must be at pains to pick out one that fits him. A very little man in a very big car is a pathetically ludicrous figure, but not more so than a very large man in a very small one. A car, in short, in which he rattles about like a grape in a drum is as obviously unsuitable to the self-respecting motorist as one in which he has to be inserted with a shoe-horn.

Before putting out the cat and setting forth to buy a car, therefore, the beginner would do well to inscribe on his cuff, or in the lining of his hat, such data as his over-all length, net tonnage, thickness (both fore-and-aft and sideways) and extent of nether limbs—or "legs", as they are termed in the vernacular. And if his is a large and heavy family, as many families are in these days of free education and tinned foodstuffs, easy to eat and rich in body-building vitamins, he will find it helpful to take with him a set of sandbags equivalent to their gross weight, so that he can test the springs of the selected vehicle without interrupting his dear ones at their daily tasks.

It is rather odd, incidentally, to reflect that the average motorist has no idea what he looks like at the wheel. Now and again, as he burns up the turnpike in his efforts to reach his favourite milk bar before closing time, he passes other drivers whose appearance strikes

For Internal Comfort

him as mirth-provoking, but it seldom occurs to him that *he* may look just as comic to them, if not more so. In other words, a man who would scorn to buy a pair of trousers that neither fitted nor became him will cheerfully buy a car that accords ill with his personality and physique and gets him considerably giggled at.

To avoid this error, the novice is advised to employ an arrangement of mirrors, as illustrated, so that he can study his reflection from the driving-seat and, when he has recovered from the shock, decide to buy some other kind of car. When carrying out this test, he should remember that as mirrors operate, so to speak, in reverse, his left ear, etc., will appear to be on the right side of his head, etc., and make allowances accordingly, as some people look even funnier from the left than from the right, and per contra, and also that to use distorting mirrors for this purpose, with the idea of making himself laugh and forget his financial worries, is to defeat the object of the experiment.

The Colour Question, which has so complicated Eastern politics for so many years, has its problems for the car buyer, too, especially if his wife is a woman of refinement and taste—as what wife is not? Nowadays cars can be had in a wide variety of colours, ranging from Purity white to Depression black, and there is no quicker method of irking the Little Woman than to choose one that clashes with her complexion or her new Spring *ensemble*.

Judging Artistic Effect Before Purchase

Choosing a Car to Match Your Wife's Complexion

As Little Women, when irked, are apt to say, do and even throw things that they afterwards regret, the car buyer who likes a quiet life is urged to take his wife along and match her, as it were. Even if no model is available in her most becoming colours, it is a fairly simple matter to have an ordinary red, white or blue one repainted in elephant's-blush (pink), Channel-crossing (green), dawn-over-Harringay (cerise), or whatever modish tint is best calculated to enhance the beauty of her eyes and draw attention to her amusing six-piece motor-suit in reversible wren's-egg nutsack (with the new inspissated gussets and a row of wooden buttons down the back).

To those unfortunates whose wives are car-conscious, clothes-crazy *and* colour-blind we have no suggestions to offer; but there cannot be many such, in this day and age.

Nobody regrets it more than we do, but it is undeniable that quite a few potential motorists are not on frightfully good terms with their wives. This is not necessarily the fault of either party; digestive troubles or incompatability of temperament—as when the wife likes wireless comedians and the husband prefers spinach—may be to blame. But where this atmosphere exists, the choice of a car is no easy matter, since any model at which She casts a yearning glance will be instantly sneered at by Him. Or vice versa, in most cases.

To meet this difficulty, Mr. Heath Robinson—as big-hearted an altruist as ever gave a beggar half a crown in the belief that it was a penny—has devised the Duocar, or Incompatobile, here shown. Briefly, this design (which can also be cut out, mounted on vellum and used as a novelty lamp-shade) not only enables any two varieties of coachwork to be combined on one chassis, but precludes the exchange of connubial chit-chat by their occupants.

Testing a New Car for Width of Garage Door

Naturally, the Incompatobile is slightly more expensive than a standard type of body, but those whose nerve-centres are beginning to turn black at the edges under the strain of continual bickering will find it well worth the extra cost.

The foregoing remarks apply chiefly to new cars, but much the same problems arise where second-hand vehicles are concerned. In the case of a second-hand car however, its colour is really of less importance than its ability, or otherwise, to go. In other words, the man who buys a used car because it blends harmoniously with his old school braces, without first satisfying himself that it can be wound up and made to tick, must be nearly as big a fool as he almost certainly looks.

To ascertain if the bodywork of a used car is in reasonably good repair, it is only necessary to creep up behind it and shake it suddenly. If anything falls off, it is probably not worth the price asked. (It is probably not worth it, anyway, but a certain

The Duo-Car for the Incompatible

HOW TO CHOOSE A CAR

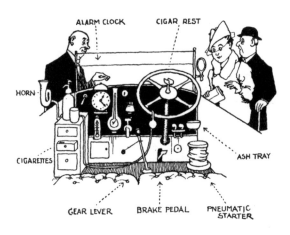

Salesman Explaining the Controls to a Possible Purchaser

margin is usually allowed for the genteel haggling which is so enjoyable a feature of these transactions.)

To find out if it actually *moves*, however (and if so, how), a Trial Run is essential. And as a short ramble round the adjacent houses is no true test of an internal-combustion engine, the wise car buyer will arrange that this demonstration occurs on a day when he has a parcel of fish to deliver in a remote parish or an aged relative to convey to a distant Home of Rest.

He should organize his itinerary, too, so that it includes at least one ploughed field (or a by-pass under repair, as the majority of by-passes are), a deepish water-splash, any other such obstacles that occur to him, and a suitable site for the all-

41

The Egg Test for Brakes

important brake test. For this last, as the illustration shows, all he needs is a hill (e.g. Primrose, Blackheath, Haverstock, etc.), an egg (obtainable at any grocer's), and a pretty steady nerve (for this, try "Peppo", 3S. 6d. and 5S., of all druggists). If the car sheds not more than four of its component parts during this searching try-out, he can confidently offer about 60 per cent of the price asked for it.

Just one thing more, and then we can go to the pictures. Many motorists with unusually full quivers are rather perturbed by the scarcity of cars large enough to accommodate their entire brood, since nothing looks worse than a bunch of kids clinging to the roof or lashed to the luggage-grid. For the benefit of such, Mr. Heath Robinson has designed the Expandocar, which is here depicted.

The "Expandocar"

This attractive model is built on the opera-hat principle, a simple movement of a lever causing the centre section to contract (as when all the children are abed with mumps) or expand (as when the whole family, plus Aunt Emily, from Goole, has to be conveyed to the Zoo). This operation should not be carried out when the car is actually in motion, as the shock is liable to detach the forecastle completely from the stern quarters, with laughable, and quite possibly, fatal, results.

Expanded

Celebrating the Payment of the Last Instalment

Well, that, in Mr. Heath Robinson's opinion—which resembles mine as closely as a whitebait resembles its twin—is about all that can usefully be said to aid the would-be motorist in the first stage of the game. If he has thoroughly absorbed our advice and carefully studied our numerous and costly diagrams, he should now be quite competent to buy a car in which his creditors at least will be surprised and annoyed to see him in.

The New Zip-opening Bonnet

*The New Rear Wheel Gear for Turning the Car
in One Movement*

HOW TO DRIVE A CAR

There is clearly not much point in owning a car unless
one can make it go. Indeed, the Government, in
its inscrutable wisdom, has decreed that anybody
found driving a car without first having learned how
to do so shall be arraigned before the Bench and
so thoroughly ticked off that his ears are likely to

burst into flames. This, of course, is as it should be, an ineptly controlled automobile being a menace to all. As it happens, Mr. Heath Robinson and I are not skilled engineers—though I can open a tin of peaches with the best, while his mastery of the corkscrew is much admired by the local Dorcas Society—but we feel it our duty to expound the basic principles of driving to the reader, so that (if he can keep awake a little longer) he will at least have a vague idea of what he is supposed to do when he sets out, all pink with apprehension and breathing loudly through his nose, to undergo his vital Test.

Having climbed into the driving-seat and peered searchingly about, the beginner will be surprised to notice three mushroom-like projections on the floor at his feet. Reading from left to right, these are the pedals operating the clutch, the brake and the accelerator; and for clarity's sake we will refer to them henceforth as "Heloise", "Abelard", and "Gladstone". To his left and/or right, according to the lay-out of the car, he will observe with interest two upright, poker-like gadgets, one being the gear-lever ("Marshall") and the other the brake-lever ("Snelgrove").

To set the car in motion, the driver must first depress Heloise with his right foot and jiggle Marshall about until it seems to click somewhere. The car is then "in gear", as we old-timers say. It is then only necessary to apply the right golosh—gently, gently!—to Gladstone, at the same time easing Snelgrove forward. If nothing happens, as is more than likely at his first essay, the driver should blush slightly and switch on the ignition—that thing like the key of a rabbit-hutch, protruding from the dashboard. That done, and the motions gone through again (Heloise, Marshall, Gladstone, Snelgrove—remember?), the car will move forward, probably with a sickening leap that may dislocate a few vertebrae. Abelard plays no part in starting the car, but will be found jolly useful for stopping it.

The driver's responsibilities do not, however, end there. Before the car can be said to be really going, he must tread rapidly on Heloise and wiggle Marshall again. When he has done this three times in all, to the accompaniment of appalling grinding noises, the car will be in "top gear", where it may remain until it meets a hill, when the whole dreary business must be repeated, only downwards. To reverse the car, the driver just joggles Marshall until it finds its appropriate niche, and then steps on Gladstone and hopes for the best, while endeavouring to look ahead, astern and sideways simultaneously.

The mechanical processes that take place during this gear-changing ritual are too involved for me to explain in the brief space at my disposal; nor does Mr. Heath Robinson know a thing about them, either. The reader (if he is still there) must just accept my personal guarantee that they *do* occur, and that if he behaves as suggested above, the results will be as indicated. More than that, I feel, cannot be expected of me.

So far, so good, as the balloonist remarked on entering the stratosphere. It is not enough, however, to know how to goad an automobile into action; the veriest moron, after all, can pull, jiggle, push and step on things until something happens. Until he has learned to *control* his vehicle when in motion, the motorist is little better than a social pest, meet only to be scooped in

by the gendarmerie and hurled into the hoosegow—
as he will be, believe us.

In his early days at the wheel, the fledgling motorist
is very apt to collide with things that abrade his
bodywork, impair his paint and do his wings no good.
To overcome this tendency, he is recommended to
put in an hour's daily steering-practice in his garden
in the manner illustrated here. The apparatus shown
comprises merely a kitchen-table, the lid of a water-
butt, a hired steering-wheel, a willing accomplice (of
either sex), three yards of stout twine and a wheeled
toy filched from the nursery. With the aid of this simple
but not uncomely machine the beginner can soon
train himself to avoid any sudden obstacle, from a

Learning to Avoid Obstacles

The New Safety Street for Learners

runaway duck to a battalion of Territorials, that he may encounter on the road.

In this connection, the attention of novice motorists who live in a quiet neighbourhood and are on good terms with their fellow-residents is drawn to Mr. Heath Robinson's design for a "Learner's Lane", which is now under consideration by the Minister of Agriculture, to whom it was sent by mistake. With a little co-operation from the neighbours and a few borrowed mattresses,

50

almost any suburban thoroughfare can be converted into a "safety street" in which the tyro can practice coming, going, turning and reversing at no risk of damaging municipal property or his own neck. The mattressed policeman is a particularly happy touch that lends verisimilitude to what might otherwise appear a mere Utopian dream. Where expense is no object, a scale-model jay-walker in some seasoned wood, fitted with a strong spring and operated (see diagram overleaf) by clockwork or a kindly friend, can be used to impress on the beginner that pedestrians do the oddest things for even odder reasons.

A point to be borne in mind by every motorist who wishes to keep out of the cemetery is that Britain's highways are free to travellers of all sorts—quite apart from pedestrians, who are simply all over the place. It is the duty, therefore, of every road-user— and of the motorist in particular, as he uses roads

Learning How to Bring On an Overtaking Car

considerably faster than, say, the muleteer or the bath-chairman—to remember that any sudden, unheralded manoeuvre on his part is liable to disorganize the traffic.

For this reason a system of signals has been devised whereby the motorist can indicate to anybody who happens to be looking exactly what he is about to do, if he can make up his mind in time. These signals should be assiduously practised (but not in the public streets lest they give rise to slanderous gossip) until they can be performed, if need be, in the dark; and I append the more important of them, with their meanings: (1) The right arm extended horizontally: "I am about to turn right", or "What ho! A blonde on the starboard beam!"

Accustoming Learners to the Erratic Movements of Pedestrians

(2) The same arm waved vertically up and down: "I am about to go slower", or "Yoo hoo, Toots!" (3) The arm waved in a vertical circle, anti-clockwise (not an easy trick, except for the double-jointed): "I am about to turn left", or "I have to do this occasionally for my rheumatism". (4) The arm pointed vertically upwards: "I am about to stop", or "At last! At last! The Pleiades!"

"I am Going to Slow Down, or Stop"

There is also a more or less optional signal, resembling under-arm bowling in a bad light on a matting wicket in September, to inform traffic astern that it can become traffic ahead, E. & O.E. and at owner's risk. When a signal has been made and, presumably, understood, the arm should be rapidly withdrawn, as otherwise facetious passers-by may shake it cordially by the hand or hang umbrellas on it.

As all these signals are made with the right hand and arm—the left being reserved for hailing friends, manipulating sandwiches, steering the car, etc.—they tend in time to overdevelop the muscles on that side of the body and impart a slightly warped appearance to the motorist. At the request of the Ministry of Health, therefore, most modern cars are fitted with little automatic direction-indicators, which flip out at the touch of a switch and light up in the prettiest way. But these gadgets—like the only sons of wealthy and indulgent mothers—are rather apt to go wrong, and the beginner is advised to rely chiefly on the manual system in emergencies.

Unusually stupid car-owners (for there is no evidence to show that motorists, as a class, are more intelligent than egg-importers or any other body of men) may find it difficult to practice traffic-signals without a little something to jazz up their imagination. As the illustrations show, this is easily arranged with the help of a few old school chums and some simple home-made props; and the occasion can even be regarded as a novel kind of party, tea and buns being served during the rehearsal and a good time had by all.

"I Want to Turn to the Left"

Teaching the Meaning of Hand Signals Made by the Car in Front

It may be argued (for some people will argue about anything, from the precise whereabouts of Atlantis to the best way of taming a zebra) that in this chapter we have not gone very deeply into the more vital aspects of motor-driving; but the truth is that we have gone into them as deeply as we know how. Fortunately for us, however, the modern car is so ably designed that it only needs starting, stopping and steering; and the motorist, provided he knows how to perform these acts without causing annoyance to the police, injury to property or anguish to members of the public, need not worry about why he does what he does when he does it.

In other words, once the driver is on terms of easy familiarity with Heloise, Abelard, Gladstone, Marshall, old Uncle Snelgrove and all, his car will move; why it moves need not concern him at the moment. How it moves, on the other hand—i.e., whether in a refined and gentlemanly manner, or like a ravening beast—is very much his affair; but as that really comes under the heading of "Road Sense, etc.", it will be dealt with later, probably under the heading of "Road Sense, etc."

Be that as it may, the beginner who commits this chapter to memory and recites it daily in his bath will appreciably hasten the approach of that happy day when he can tear the shameful "L" from his horseless carriage and—alone, care-free and unafraid—become an integral factor in Britain's Traffic Problem.

And what, apart from a double helping of fresh asparagus, could be nicer than that?

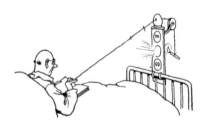

Comfortable Way of Learning About Traffic Lights

Temporary Repairs to a Buckled Wing

MAINTENANCE AND SIMPLE REPAIRS

Racing-Camels, tomato-plants and motor-cars have at least one point of resemblance: if they are to give of their best, unstintingly and at all times, they must be carefully housed and looked after. In other words, a car that is left out in the open all the year round, unwashed, unoiled, ungreased, at the mercy of every passing tempest and freely nested in by casual hens, etc., will not—nay, cannot—function as efficiently as one that gets its due meed of roofage and lubrication.

Although most modern homes are fitted with car-accommodation, the garageless house is not yet obsolete; and the latter's tenant is often at a loss to know where to keep his horseless carriage, particularly if his garden is so small—as many gardens are—that his hollyhocks have to lean sideways to let his rhubarb come up. A garage over which the tradesmen have

A Convenient Garage

to climb when delivering merchandise is more of a nuisance than an asset, as is one that has to be bodily removed whenever the gardener wishes to prune the antirrhinums. In such cases an obvious solution is a simple hoistable garage (see diagram), which costs little to erect, can be neatly skyed when not in use, and lends a pleasant touch of *bizarrerie* to the messuage. (Look that word up for yourselves. I had to.)

Even simpler, cheaper and more amusing to operate is the "Expandokarkosi" which Mr. Heath Robinson invented while playing his accordion one evening in January last. This, as the illustration shows, consists of a waterproof canvas covering on a sort of "lazy-tongs" framework which is fitted with pointed steel legs and permanently attached to the car by nuts of rustless steel: and it is as easy to work as it is fascinating to watch.

A suitable site having been selected (that is, within easy strolling distance of those major necessities of Life, a tavern, a pawnbroker and a tobacconist) and the car brought to rest, a movement of a lever lowers the aforesaid legs and thrusts them firmly into the ground. On the cry "All clear aft!" the car is caused slowly to reverse, thus expanding the framework and *garaging itself as it goes*. Snails, of course, put themselves up for the night in a very similar way; but to imbue an inanimate bit of machinery with this spirit of independence is no small achievement on Mr. Heath Robinson's part.

The garage problem settled by one or other of these expedients, the question of the car's maintenance rears its ugly head. On being reminded by some

The Portable Garage

Greasing the Car in One Movement

officious busybody that it is high time he greased and/ or oiled and/or washed his car, the normal motorist is apt to wilt visibly and change the subject, but to neglect these nauseous tasks is to risk being immobilized by a seized toggle-gasket-valve on a lonely road in the middle of the night and a temper.

It is only when he comes to grease his car that the motorist realizes how much of it there is, and how little of it is accessible. And as crawling all over it with a grease-gun, stabbing profanely at the chassis and sustaining abrasions, is hardly anybody's idea of fun, the attention of those interested is respectfully drawn to the alternative here depicted. By this method, as the illustration shows, the car can be cajoled into lubricating itself, the necessary apparatus comprising only a lot of rubber gas-tubing, a few citizens of ample physique, and a large, second-hand concertina from which the din has been removed. By filling the concertina with grease, attaching the tubing to strategic points about the car, and assembling the citizens on the back seat, the healing lubricant can be forced into the remotest corners of the vehicle in rather less time than it takes to get married, fry an egg, or lose a fortune on the Turf.

Washing the car is a somewhat easier job, though fraught with peril for the rheumatic. It is not enough, however, merely to stand afar off and hurl water at it from a bucket; the cleansing fluid must be applied with care—and preferably with a powerful hose—if it is to achieve its object. Where no powerful hose is available, a common (or garden) watering-can, or even a strong fountain-pen-filler or scent-spray, can be employed in lieu.

Only the indecently rich, by the way, use rose-water, or water specially imported from Killarney, for; this purpose. For the modern mass-produced car ordinary H_2O, obtainable from any tap, is quite good enough. In time of drought, and in districts afflicted with a high water-rate, the motorist can economize slightly by washing his car only on Saturday nights and compelling his family—clad in bathing-suits and carrying their own soap—to gather in and around it while he does so.

So much for that, and not one syllable more. A few words, now, about certain simple running-repairs (so-called because they are invariably done at the halt) which every car-owner should know how to execute, no matter how costly his car or how great his reluctance to get his hands dirty. As has been pointed out elsewhere, the car of today rarely breaks down, blows up, caves in or falls apart; but it does occasionally come to a standstill for no apparent reason.

Cleaning the car

The Portable Petrol Pump

The most common cause of these sudden stoppages is a shortage of petrol, the sap at the wheel having forgotten to replenish the tank. The remedy for this is a brisk walk to the nearest filling-station; but as this may easily entail a five-mile trudge o'er fen and marsh and lea, with a two-gallon petrol-tin agonizing the dexter bicep, the motorist will find it a good plan to carry his own personal petrol-pump in the manner here shown. Affixed to the side of the car and fed from a reserve supply secreted beneath the chassis, this handy accessory can be painted to resemble a golf-bag—just to fool the public—and worn flat on the running-board when not required.

Equally effective in stopping a car, and far more serious in its after-effects, is a sudden shortage of water. On seeing dense clouds of steam issue from the radiator, to the accompaniment of an eerie bubbling noise, it is advisable to halt and let the vehicle simmer down, even if it makes one late for tea with an affluent aunt in Dulwich. Denied a regular water-supply, car-engines get red hot and fall out on the road in a molten mass, quite pretty to look at but useless for propulsive purposes. The car-owner who likes to prepare for all contingencies, therefore, is urged to carry an auxiliary water-tank from which the radiator can be re-filled as necessary by means of a piston operated from and by the driving-seat, as illustrated. Apart from its value as an anti-calamity influence, this device is a boon to footballers and others who wish to develop their calf muscles.

If investigation reveals an abundance of petrol in the tank, no foreign substance—such as a fragment of granite, a dead moth, or the unconsumed portion

For Filling Up with Water without Stopping

of a ham-sandwich—in the carburettor, and a lot of water in the radiator, the motorist must systematically examine the vital parts of the engine until he tracks the trouble to its source.

To do this, he may have to unscrew, peer at, blow through and fiddle with a variety of bits and pieces; and these should be carefully replaced as he goes along, if he can remember whence they came. There is no more pitiable figure than the man who, in his determination to cure his car's *malaise*, reduces it practically to its component parts, only to find on re-assembling it that he has several weirdly shaped and unaccountable bits left over.

If the trouble is in the ignition-system, the motorist is advised to hire a horse and tow the car to the nearest garage, as fooling about with voltages, etc., is a job for experts. In fact, almost everything that goes wrong with a car is a job for experts, as unskilled tampering with the machinery is liable to do more harm than good. True, there *are* car-owners who do all their own repairs, and who are never happier than when re-stabilizing a fused crankshaft or fitting a new plunger-socket to a differential; but it is not for the benefit of such that this work has been written, printed and registered at Fishmongers' Hall as third-class giggle-matter.

Although many modern car-owners live out their days without ever experiencing a puncture, tyres do go flat occasionally, forcing the motorist to utter an unmuffled oath, climb out and change the wheel. Wheel-changing, though a simple enough operation, is one of Life's more irksome tasks, as it involves considerable effort with a jack and a wheel-brace and

The Cause of All the Trouble:
The Mouse in the Magneto

leaves the hands richly begrimed, the nerve-fibres badly frayed and the braces seriously strained.

The motorist who dislikes that sort of thing—and the motorist who doesn't ought to have his head examined—might do worse than equip his car with a Heath Robinson "Rôdswêp Tyahsavah". As the diagram explains, this is a stout rotary brush of sterilized warthog-bristles, attached to the prow of the car and string-operated from the driving-seat on the appearance of a tintack or a broken bottle on the fairway. This gadget is dedicated with love and best wishes to the Anti-Litter League, as it not only scoops unsightly jetsam off the road but deposits it in a tray under the radiator, whence it can be removed at leisure and sold for what it will fetch.

A rather more expensive doohickus for the use of those whose spare wheel is in hock or who are loth to get out and heave is the "Eveready Fifthwheel", also depicted here. This is merely a solid-tyred castor at the end of a hinged lever which can be lowered in the wink of an eye when a loud "ping"

For Preserving the Tyres

The Ever Ready Fifth Wheel

and the sinister whistle of escaping air indicates that it is needed. A car fitted with two of these dinguses can sustain punctures in all four wheels and still be driven fast enough—on the mono-rail principle, of course—to reach the "Archdeacon's Arms" before closing time.

In addition to the spanners, tyre-levers, and what-nots supplied by the manufacturers, it is a good idea to carry a few extra tools and simple comforts that may or may not prove helpful in a crisis. Neither Mr. Heath Robinson nor I, for example, would drive a yard in any direction without our Emergency Kit, which is a small sandalwood box with two entwined hearts pokerworked on the lid, and containing:

A corkscrew (for extracting any corks that may get embedded in the tyres).

Some assorted string (for lashing things to things).

A hairpin (for cleaning pipes, carburettor-jets, etc.).

Four drawing-pins (for securing the roof of the car in hurricanes).

Some wire-netting (for fitting over the exhaust-pipe to keep out stoats when parked in primeval woodland).

A packet of pemmican (for eating when stranded by engine-trouble in Glasgow on a Sunday).

Some rope (for being towed with).

A little green china elephant with red eyes (for luck).

A bottle of light ale (for fun).

With the aid of a few such properties, the statutory tool-kit and the hints hereinbefore set forth, the motorist whose car stops inexplicably should be able, if not actually to make it go again, at least to irritate it slightly. And if all else fails, he can either push it to the nearest garage, leave it by the wayside and run to his destination, or give it away in a fit of pique to the first passer-by.

Frankly, it is all one to us.

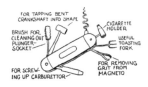

The Motorists Companion

For the Cause of Art

ROAD SENSE AND ETIQUETTE

A man—or a woman, for that matter—is not necessarily a good motorist because he/she can handle a car with nonchalant ease and make it do everything but dance the hornpipe. Such technical dexterity helps, of course; but it is chiefly by his/her deportment on the road that he/she will be judged. And as such judging is apt to be done by magistrates (many of them fitted with an anti-auto complex and quite old enough to have been patted on the head by George IV) in a manner that leaves a bad dent in the judgee's pocket-book, it behoves every car-owner to watch his step as carefully as if it owed him money.

Very useful in this respect is the indefinable faculty known as "road-sense", which, roughly, is the ability to guess what is likely to happen twenty seconds hence and five hundred yards away. Some drivers never acquire this knack, but continue to collide with things at irregular intervals throughout their motoring life, to their surprise and indignation. The majority, however, sooner or later learn by experience to foresee possible calamity and act accordingly.

On sighting a hen or a policeman, for example, the road-sensible motorist instinctively slows down (or up). Hens, having no road- (or any other) sense, will work themselves into a frenzy in their efforts to get run over: and no car can be regarded as fully under control that has a Rhode Island Red entangled in the steering-gear. As for policemen, these, as a class, are kindly, sunny-natured chaps, clean in their habits, courteous to the aged poor, and kitten-lovers to a man; but they have their duty to perform.

Thoughtful Motorist

Road Sense

True, a cop on the skyline does not invariably portend disaster, for the regulations governing motoring in England are so many and various that not even a policeman can possibly remember them all. Nevertheless, it is as well to play for safety and cruise past the constabulary at not more than 15 m.p.h., bowing affably to it in passing. Though it will probably not respond, it will appreciate the gesture. (A policeman on duty, by the way, should not be offered buns, asked riddles or otherwise hampered in his work; but there is no harm in trying to win his love by leaving some simple gift—a pot of tea, say, a posy of wall-flowers or an improving book—where he will find it when he knocks off for the day.)

Hens and constables apart, the motorist who keeps his eyes open—after all, he will not be a motorist long if he persists in keeping them shut—and his wits active can avoid a lot of trouble. One need not, for example, be a professional sleuth to deduce that a gaily coloured rubber ball, bouncing suddenly into the roadway, is liable to be followed by an equally sudden and bouncing child, and should therefore be regarded as a danger-signal. In the same way, an Indian mahout, abruptly emerging from a side road, should be viewed with grave suspicion, as where there is a mahout there is very apt to be an elephant, than which there is no more damaging animal to run into.

Cyclists, of course, should always be kept well away from. On high days and holidays our main roads are alive with these brightly plumaged creatures, all pedalling furiously from here to there in order to pedal furiously back again. And very charming they look, too, with their youthful torsos curved like so many croquet-hoops and their little feet revolving at a speed to dazzle the eye. But as the modern cyclist travels, for some reason, with his frank, open countenance on a level with his shins, and is therefore rather vague as to what is going on about him, he should be given as wide a berth as circumstances

Courtesy

allow, as no car looks its best with half a bicycle and a total stranger impaled on its front dumb-irons.

Even worse than cyclists, from the point of view of one who gets embedded in them, are sheep. A wobble* of cyclists does at least move, whereas a flock of sheep merely oozes, looking like a lot of agitated aunts with acute dyspeptic trouble. On meeting sheep, the motorist's only course is to stop, fold his hands and start declining *mensa* to keep himself awake. The practice of fitting a stout rubber sheep-plough to the radiator, with the idea of cleaving a path through casual flocks, is not recommended, as it (a) annoys the shepherd and (b) does the sheep no good.

Still more exasperating to the motorist in a hurry— as most motorists seem to be—is a herd of cows,

---

* O. Eng. noun of assembly. Cf. "A wisp of snipe", "a futility of statesmen", "a penury of authors", etc.

probably because a cow's natural expression is far more contemptuous, and its reluctance to be bustled even greater, than that of the average sheep. Broadly speaking, indeed, one may say that any animal encountered on an English road is not only a nuisance but a potential danger to the motorist, no matter how dear it may be to its owner.

Preoccupation with hens, policemen, cows or cyclists, however, is no excuse for neglecting to obey the roadsigns with which the fair face of England bristles nowadays. Many of these—e.g., "HALT", "GO SLOW", "TURN LEFT", "GO SLOWER", "TURN RIGHT", "TURN ROUND", "LOSE TWO TURNS", "GO HOME AND START AGAIN", etc.—are perfectly legible, even if they do not invariably make sense; but some are in the form of impressionistic puzzle-drawings, highly entertaining to the cognoscenti but rather baffling to the foreigner. (A blazing torch, for example, betokens a nearby school, and not, as one would expect, a fire-station.)

To remedy this injustice, Mr. Heath Robinson—a keen student of immigration problems—has designed (see illustrations) a series of pictorial road-signs

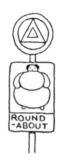

whose meaning should be instantly apparent to the dumbest alien. This, I may add, he has done with no thought of personal gain or any hope that anything will come of it, though in the unlikely event of the Ministry of Transport adopting his suggestions he would not, I think, refuse a small honorarium, or knighthood.

Quite apart from his duty to the State, the car-owner who wishes to avoid collisions, recriminations and possibly even fisticuffs should behave towards his fellow-motorists with unswerving courtesy. The common road-hog, or greater pimpled *motorbeeste*, is not yet quite extinct, though large numbers are trapped every year; but it is now pretty generally realized by the motoring-classes that Politeness Pays.

After all, the fact that he is entirely surrounded by a motor-car on which he has probably paid only a few instalments is no reason why a man should neglect the ordinary decencies of life. It does not, for one thing, absolve him from the obligation of tipping his lid to chance-met feminine acquaintances. Many drivers are opposed to hat-raising in such circumstances, on the ground that it involves removing a hand from the wheel and an eye from the road and thus risking a collision with whatever there is to collide with. But this difficulty, can easily be overcome by cutting a small trapdoor in the roof of the car (as shown in the illustration below) through which the hat can be brandished at the passing fair, with or without a sidelong glance, by means of a small lever and a piece of twine worked by the driver's foot (or passenger, if any).

Re sidelong glances, by the way. These should rarely be indulged in by the conscientious driver, as they may easily cause trouble, particularly if the person glanced at is a comely member of what, in those dear, dead days when women wore their own complexions and hats that were recognizable as such, was known as the "Fair Sex". Love (the little rogue) is no respecter of traffic problems, and the motorist's natural reaction, on being struck by Cupid's dart, is to wrench convulsively at the wheel and run into something.

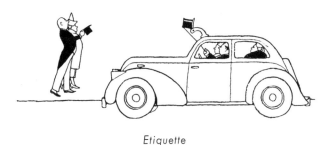

Etiquette

Love at First Sight

Well, if what he runs into is the comely member, all may turn out for the best, as more than one romance has burgeoned in a Cottage Hospital. If, on the other hand, it is the local reservoir or a passing pantechnicon, he will probably regret his *lapsus oculi* (I think).

In the same way, and for much the same reason, it is dashed bad form to overtake a blonde fellow-motorist on a blind corner, or to cut-in on her in such a way as to edge her into the ditch. Cars wearing large crimson "L"s and driven, more or less, by typical Englishwomen should be treated with profound respect, as nobody—and least of all, as a rule, the typical Englishwomen—can foretell what they are likely to do next. In fact, and to beat about no more bushes, the male motorist's attitude towards she-drivers of all ages should be one of flawless but rather distant courtesy, tinged slightly with apprehension.

Deciding the Right of Way

HOW TO BE A MOTORIST

Mr. Heath Robinson, incidentally, is of the opinion that policemen on point-duty like to have their outstretched hands shaken occasionally by passing she-motorists, and especially by Beauty Queens, Glamour Girls and similar compelling eyefuls. My own view, however, is that this intimacy is permissible only when the policeman is a *personal friend* of the motorist and can be trusted to accept the pleasantry in the spirit in which it is offered. Otherwise, it seems to me, he may get the wrong idea, suspect that he is being got at, blow his whistle, draw his truncheon and start reaching for his handcuffs. And I, personally, wouldn't blame him.

It sometimes happens (for almost anything can happen nowadays, and there are few things that do not) that four motorists converge simultaneously from four different directions—such as N., S., E., and W.—upon a cross-roads, and there pause in mutual doubt as to which has the right of way. Where all four are of an equally yielding disposition and unwilling to claim precedence, the resultant deadlock is liable to paralyse all traffic within a five-mile radius. In these cases the best solution is to draw lots for the privilege of proceeding, and preferably from a policeman's helmet; but if no such headwear is available, almost any old hat will do.

So much for road-sense, by-pass etiquette, arterial manners and the best method of keeping sheep out of your carburettor. In the limited space at our disposal it is impossible for us to cover every aspect of this matter; but if the foregoing suggestions enable even one (1) motorist to do the right thing at the right time on even one (1) occasion, we shall feel that our labours have not been entirely in vain.

There Is No More Damaging Animal To Run Into

The Hat Bulge

SPECIAL BODIES

Like molluscs, Members of Parliament, misogynists and moths, motor-cars vary considerably in shape. There are, indeed, so many different types of body-work on the market that it would take two grown men and a smallish boy at least half an hour to describe them all.

Nevertheless, there are bound to be a few ultra-fastidious motorists who can find no car exactly suited to their needs, and who are too busy, too lazy or just too darned bone-headed to design one for themselves. And to these—although, mark you, they have never done a thing for *us*—we offer the following suggestions, with the accompanying blue-prints, which cover almost every aspect of this problem in a logical and scholarly manner.

In the life of every motorist there are moments (e.g. when he sights a ravening creditor in the offing or remembers that he has left the baby running loose at home) when he has to stop suddenly, turn quickly and go back. Generally, this entails a certain amount of reversing, a time-wasting manoeuvre that not every driver is either keen on or good at. For the benefit of reluctant reversers, Mr. Heath Robinson has designed the "Twosnout" double-ended car-body, which (see diagram below) is fitted with twin steering-wheels, two sets of lights, and no fewer than four windscreen-wipers.

This type of coachwork needs only one engine (nestling fore or aft, as desired), and enables the driver to go to or fro with equal ease and precision, to the confusion of traffic-cops, myopic pedestrians and the like. With two drivers, naturally, even quicker results are obtainable; but the motorist who cannot afford to carry a spare self will find that leaping back and forth from seat A to seat B will greatly benefit his liver.

To the motorist who has no garage of his own, nor any wish to pay an excessive rent for an inadequate portion of somebody else's, the "Collapso" telescopic

For Reversing Quickly

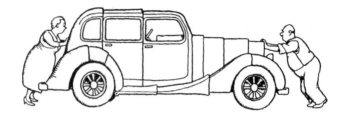

The Folding car

body should prove a boon indeed. This, as the illustration shows, is so cunningly contrived and so delicately adjusted that a slight push at the radiator causes every part of the car (except, of course, the extreme rear) to disappear into the part immediately behind it, somewhat to the surprise of anybody who happens to be watching.

When completely folded, the "Collapso" looks less like an automobile than one would believe possible, and can be wheeled about by hand, sent up and

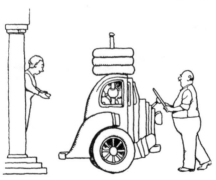

down in lifts, and housed for the night in the oddest places, such as cycle-sheds and wardrobes. If this type of body has a fault (which we are unwilling to admit), it is that when involved in a collision it is inclined to fold itself unasked, with painful consequences to its inmates; but that is a small price to pay for its many unique advantages.

Motorists who go in for picnicking—as many of them do, since the British are never so happy as when eating ill-chosen meals in a bitter wind and beneath a lowering sky—are often worried by crumbs in the carburettor, jam on the upholstery, and similar drawbacks to open-air gourmandise. An ordinary car is no place in which to eat things with any real gusto, even hard-boiled eggs having a tendency to fall about, get trodden on, and work through the floorboards into the transmission.

A glance at the accompanying diagram, however, will show that it is quite easy to adapt any modern

The Picnic Saloon

The Modesty Bathing Car

car to purposes of picnickery. If the front seats are temporarily replaced by piano-stools and a simple bench for two persons fixed to the spare wheel at the back, all the essential trenchwork can be done on the roof of the car and the unconsumed portion of the day's rations flung to passing kine, etc. In this way the driver and his human freight can more or less enjoy an *al fresco* snack in comparative comfort and without littering the interior of the car with egg-shells, salmon-tins, partially gnawed wish-bones and similar bric-a-brac.

During the summer, many picnics are staged at the seaside, to give all concerned a chance to gambol in the deep. And to those who, having no illusions about their physique, are reluctant to display it in a bathing-suit, we would recommend the Heath Robinson "Anti-Blush Autotent". This is simply a collapsible canvas tunnel which can be attached to the back of any car and fully extended in no time by anybody who knows how to do so; and through it the shyest and most oddly shaped bather can creep into and dash out of the sea in complete privacy, ungiggled-at, unsnapshotted and unashamed.

(When not needed for this humanitarian purpose, the Autotent can be detached from the car, erected in the garden, and used as a storm-proof skittle-alley, fowl-run or snail-racing track.)

The problem of keeping boredom at bay, not only at auto-picnics but on long motor journeys of all sorts,

The Sinking Body

is one that confronts every active-minded motorist; but it has been left to the over-signed (us, in other words) to solve it. As the illustration shows, the body of any car fitted with the H.R. "Qwiksynk" chassis can be lowered instantly to ground-level by a single jerk of the wrist. The roof of the car thus becomes available for a stirring bout of ping-pong (as table-tennis was aptly called before it went all high-hat), an excellent game for dispelling ingrowing lassitude, spots before the eyes, and other symptoms of ennui.

(It may be objected by the parsimonious that a far cheaper method of staying awake at the wheel is to stop the car occasionally and run briskly round in circles until insomnia sets in. True enough; but where, for Pete's sake, is the entertainment value in that?)

The fact that the modern car is a good deal wider than the old-fashioned horse is often a source of embarrassment to those who like to do their motoring in remote, uncharted by-ways, of which there are still about two dozen left in the United Kingdom. Many English lanes were designed only to accommodate the solitary horseman who figured so frequently in Victorian novels, and any vehicle broader than a perambulator is therefore liable to get stuck in them.

As there is nothing more humiliating to a sensitive motorist than to be suddenly immobilized in this way, with a lot of odorous honeysuckle intruding at one window and a whortleberry-bush menacing him at the other, Mr. Heath Robinson's agile brain (which is not only twice the size of mine, but far better-looking) has evolved the "Narrokar" for use on such excursions. Though possibly not quite slim enough to pass through the eye of a camel (a necessity, after all, that seldom arises nowadays), this model, as the drawing shows, is sufficiently attenuated to go almost anywhere else. For this reason its resemblance to a perpendicular coffin should not be held against it, because one cannot have *everything*, can one?

Obviously the "Narrokar" is suitable only for motorists who have retained that Schoolboy Outline. Those others who, through defective glands or overindulgence in quails-in-aspic, have become practically spherical, are advised to keep well away from English lanes (and from camels' eyes, for that matter) at all times; but there is no reason why they, too, should not take a hint from us. A car with concave sides—made to measure, of course—is the very thing for the incurably corpulent, as it allows them to breathe deeply without breaking the windows, and by its very globularity distracts attention from their shape.

The Narrokar

Owners of unnecessarily large cars—the kind that extend for about twelve yards in both directions and move with a sinister absence of noise—are sometimes baffled by the "roundabouts" with which the

The Bending Body for Negotiating Roundabouts

authorities have studded our main roads in the hope of persuading people to stay alive a little longer. In negotiating one of these obstacles, a very long car may find itself acting as the chord of a circle several sizes too small for it—a position not only absurd, in the Euclidean sense, but very hard to get out of gracefully. One method of overcoming this difficulty is to sell the car and buy a tricycle; and another is to have the body and chassis of the car jointed in the middle, so that it can slide round the most awkward corners in a supple, reptilian manner, very impressive to see.

So far as purely ornamental coachwork is concerned, the motorist whose means permit can go as far as he likes. Commercial vehicles in the shape of bottles, loaves, barrels, cottages and what not are familiar objects of the countryside today; and the same

90

principle can be applied to any private car. Indeed, in the interest of our national gaiety it should be so applied by every car-owner who can afford it.

In this respect, if I may say so, those Eastern potentates who buy their jewels by the ton and their cars by the gross show a sad lack of imagination. True, they usually insist on ivory steering-wheels, solid platinum gear-levers and a few other such refinements; but they do not often improve on the standard coachwork. This is regrettable, in my view, inasmuch as a car built to resemble, say, a small portion of Baghdad, with a couple of domes and a minaret and a real ruby tail-light and accommodation for the odd wife or two, would surely increase its owner's prestige and form a gratifying eyeful for his subjects.

The Harem Saloon, for Eastern Potentates

The Cathedral Body

Again, although the average British bishop is a pretty striking figure as he roams his diocese, bowing affably to all and sundry, he would look still more impressive if he did his roaming in a car specially designed to express his personality. Nothing gaudy or ostentatious is required for this; just a vaguely church-shaped vehicle with Gothic windows (for looking out of), a small but penetrating carillon (for clearing the way), a little imitation steeple, with clock inset (for telling the time), and a slight bulge in the roof (to prevent the yawl-rigged hat being rammed down over the episcopal ears by sudden bumps in the road).

These are but two examples—both perfectly feasible, as the illustrations testify—of what could be done by Britain's motorists to brighten our otherwise greyish lives and do the coachwork industry a bit of lasting good. It only remains now for the said motorists to do the right thing by us and justify our simple Norman faith; and if any of them need any help at any time, Mr. Heath Robinson and I will be only too happy to oblige, for a consideration.

The Sideways Body for the Discomfiture of Road Hogs

The Unowheel
For Reducing Tyre Troubles

ACCESSORIES

By comparison with the modern motor-car, the early horseless carriage was sold to the public in a pretty naked condition. It had a body (rather laughable in shape), an engine (guaranteed to do its stuff occasionally), and a wheel at each corner; but otherwise it was as bare of gadgets and accessories as the chariot in which Boadicea did her battling, shopping, etc. The motorist of that era who craved lamps to light him home from the "Nightshirt and Frog", or a horn wherewith to scare the peasantry out of its limited wits, had to save up and buy same for himself, often at the sacrifice of his wife's new spring toque or his children's summer holiday.

ACCESSORIES

Today, however, car manufacturers are more generously inclined. The standard fittings of the modern car, indeed, comprise almost everything except a service-lift, a binnacle and a thing for removing stones from horses' hoofs; and even these would probably be included if there were any real demand for them, or any horses.

All the same, there are certain other little refinements which add considerably to the pleasure of motoring and enable the motorist to distinguish his own car from others of the same make—not always an easy job in this age of mass-production, when cars of the same species resemble one another as closely as twins.

A case in point is the radiator mascot, which is a little model of something (of anything, in fact, from the Leaning Tower of Pisa to a taxpayer at bay) affixed to the prow of the car as a mark of respect for St. Christopher, the motorists' patron saint. Though there is no evidence to show that this emblem really helps to propitiate Fate and keep the motorist out of the police-court, it improves the appearance of the car and gives garage-hands some-thing to pull it about by. Models of storks, snipe and other sharp-nosed objects are not recommended for this purpose, as they are liable to puncture any pedestrians with whom they come in contact; but otherwise the mascot-enthusiast can let his artistic imagination rip. (A little rubber replica of the Home Secretary, for example, is both a graceful compliment to Authority and a useful emergency ink-eraser, while a small-scale reproduction, in solid granite, of Battersea Power Station or the motorist's richest aunt lends a touch of *diablerie* to any car and comes in handy for striking matches.)

No matter how rare and costly his radiator-mascot, however, the motorist who suffers from cold feet—as many do in mid-winter, though seldom (if British) in time of war—is an object of compassion, as nobody who is numb from the knees down can really get a kick out of motoring. All who tend to get that way, therefore, are obsequiously urged to study the simple central-heating system, known as the "Autophootjoye", which Mr. Heath Robinson has devised for their benefit (in his sleep, to be perfectly frank).

This, as the diagram shows, consists of a small zinc water-tank, glued to the back of the car, warmed by an inexpensive oil-stove and connected by a stout leaden pipe to a Schmultz-Bungwasser circulatory boiler slung beneath the chassis in such a position that the passengers can rest their poor, shivering feet on it through holes cut in the floorboards. An obvious advantage of this apparatus is that it works equally

Simple Home-Made Central Heating Device

ACCESSORIES

*How to Enjoy a Pipe in Comfort Without
Filling the Car with Smoke*

well in reverse—i.e. unusually hot-blooded motorists, by eliminating the oil-lamp and filling the tank with ice, can use it to keep their feet *cool*—while goldfish, tame newts and other forms of pond-life can be transported in it at no extra cost.

Mention of leaden pipes reminds me, by a curious association of ideas, that men who smoke odorous old briars, clays and meerschaums in motor-cars are rarely popular with their fellow-passengers. To avoid being reproachfully wheezed at by the latter, it is a good plan to have a special stormproof pipe permanently clamped to the roof of the car and smoke it through a flexible tube, as shown in the illustration.

This dodge, which is an adaption of the well-known Turkish "hookah" and was revealed to Mr. Heath Robinson in a dream by a Levantine rabbit-fancier whom he saved from drowning in the Bosphorus, allows the noxious fumes to escape, leave the inmates of the car unstupefied, and imparts a pleasing touch of *je-ne-sais-quoi* to the vehicle.

Cigarette-smokers who motor a lot are often uncertain how to dispose of their cigarette-ends; and the same applies to motorists who smoke a lot of cigarettes. The ash-trays supplied with the average car are very apt to overflow, while to hurl the unconsumed portion of the day's smoking from the window is to disfigure the countryside and risk blinding in-offensive passers-by. *External* ash-trays, mounted on tasteful wrought-iron brackets and worked from within the car by short pieces of coloured tape, are the obvious solution of this difficulty, as small pots of geraniums can be carried in them, with a delightfully decorative effect, in the event of the car-owner being forced to give up smoking for his health or by his wife.

Many people who like motoring are also keen on card-games; but until Mr. Heath Robinson brought

External Ash-trays

The Rising Floor for Bridge Players

"Cyclops", his giant intellect, to bear on the matter it was not possible to engage in both these pastimes simultaneously. Now, however, merely by cutting out a section of the rear floorboards and fitting it with telescopic legs contrived from four old telescopes, the card-minded motorist and his companions can enjoy a stimulating game of "Snap" or "Find-the-Lady" almost anywhere between John's End and Land o' Groats. And when this palls, or one of the party has lost more than he can afford and gone home in a tram and a huff, a cold collation can be served on the extempore card-table and partaken of with enthusiasm.

Not once or twice in his rough island story, every motorist finds it necessary to stop and ask somebody the way to somewhere. More often than not, this gets him nowhere, the person asked proving to be a stranger in those parts; but on the rare occasions when

The Tipping Tube

the required information is forthcoming in an accent that can be understood, it is a kindly act to requite the informant with a small sum in bronze.

Unfortunately, the modern streamlined car is so close-fitting that no driver who has outgrown his childhood can get at his pockets without a struggle that imposes a severe strain on his braces and may even dislocate his neck. The attention of all motorists whose generosity is stronger than their sense of direction, therefore, is respectfully drawn to an ingenious device, here depicted, whereby largesse can be showered, coin by coin, upon the populace with the minimum of exertion. By the adjustment of a butterfly-nut this gadget can be adapted to issue banknotes (on behalf of motorists with more money than sense) or temperance tracts (for those having neither sense nor money).

It sometimes happens that a short-sighted or dull-witted driver, on being suddenly confronted by a point-duty cop at an unfamiliar cross-roads, is at a loss to interpret the flail-like gestures of the man in blue.

ACCESSORIES

Our British policemen are notoriously wonderful, but they vary a good deal in shape, and some are naturally better than others at directing traffic in mime. They all have their pride, however, and are inclined to resent being peevishly shouted at by motorists unacquainted with the local tic-tac code.

To preserve harmony on such occasions, the car-owner who is not very quick in the uptake might do a lot worse than carry on the bows of his car a large model query-mark in solid tin or weatherproofed mahogany, worked by a piece of string from the driving-seat and signifying in any language: "*Pardon. Kindly repeat and/or elucidate.*" Much time that might otherwise be wasted in mutual recriminations can be saved by this

To Indicate a Doubt as to the Next Move

For Detecting Bubbling Sounds in the Radiator

simple dingus, which costs little to instal and gives the front of the car an appealingly wistful look.

Not every motorist, of course, is either deaf or dull-witted, the majority, indeed, being remarkably quick to hear and react to the age-old question: "What's yours?" But only the most experienced are sufficiently alert-eared to detect those small, sinister sounds with which an internal-combustion engine announces that all is not well with it, and that it is liable to blow up at any moment.

Well, that is where an ordinary medical stethoscope comes in very useful. Employed in the manner shown, with the receiving end in the radiator and the ear-pieces attached to the driver, it magnifies and transmits to the latter all unusual bubblings, clankings, rattles, squeaks and similar portents of disaster, thus warning him to stop, alight and do something about it before the worst befalls.

I come now, rather diffidently, to a couple of suggestions of which Mr. Heath Robinson thinks pretty highly, but which I—pompous old prig that I am

—consider slightly anti-social. Still, what will be, will be (well, won't it?), and presumably it is our duty as public benefactors to cater for all tastes, including those of the Underworld. After all, many smash-and-grab practitioners are enthusiastic motorists—in fact, to the persistent pincher of other persons' property a well-equipped car is essential.

Hence the ingenious accessory which Mr. Heath Robinson has evolved—under an assumed name, for obvious reasons—for collectors of bric-a-brac who have never known the refining influence of a good woman's love. This apparatus consists merely of an expanding metal arm, two bits of string and a brick, and can be fitted to any make of car by anybody with an atrophied conscience.

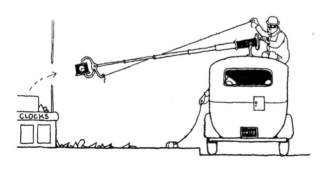

Illegal Accessories

Purloining Power

Ever ready to assist the under-dog, and mildly annoyed—as who isn't?—by the high price of petrol, Mr. Heath Robinson has also worked out a scheme (of which no true Vicar could approve) whereby the impoverished motorist can run his car on electricity at the expense of the local trolley-bus company. The accompanying drawing is nearly as self-explanatory as the impoverished motorist will have to be if anybody catches him at it. That, however, is *his* affair, and nobody can say we didn't warn him.

The reader who has kept his head and reached this point without succumbing to ennui, sleep, or a craving to go to the movies, will have realized, we hope, that the intelligent use of string can do much to improve the appearance and performance of any motor-car. Where no string is available, twine, tape, or even plaited *bimbo-grass* (which grows only on the

Patagonian plains in alternate Leap Years) can be utilized instead; but the principle—"a knot here, a knot there, and save what's left over"—remains the same.

Keen string-fanciers to a man, Mr. Heath Robinson and I hold pretty strong views about this valuable, inexpensive and under-estimated commodity. And if our joint efforts to make Britain thoroughly string-conscious meet with only half the success they deserve, we shall feel that we have not half-lived in vain.

The Anti-Vibration Seat

The "Home From Home" Caravan

FOREIGN TOURING AND CARAVAN LIFE

The urge to take his car abroad for a spell, thus Getting Away From It All, is one that attacks every motorist occasionally, usually after a heavy meal of cold boiled pork or on learning that his richest aunt has left her all to a Cats' Home. If he is by nature timorous, he may be deterred from obeying this impulse by his ignorance of alien tongues, his fear of foreign foodstuffs and his suspicion that all foreigners —apart, of course, from the enlightened few who play cricket—are raffish, rascally, rapacious and (in Russia) razorless.

Well—to beat about no bushes—the purpose of this chapter is to show that such qualms are unjustified, and that, from the escapist point of view, the Continent unquestionably has the bulge on England, which is relatively so small that Getters-Away-From-It-All frequently fall over the edge. The language difficulty, for example, scarcely exists today, for although it is certainly startling to hear quite small French children speaking fluent French with almost insolent ease, it will be found that most of their elders have a nodding acquaintance with what they assume to be English.

As for foreign food, it should suffice to say that foreigners have been eating it for years, and yet manage to survive in large numbers. In *re* their alleged eagerness to denude the stranger in their midst of everything but his underwear, it has yet to be proved that this is greater than that of certain English landladies whom it would be discourteous: (though salutary) to name.

About the only real difficulty, in fact, which confronts the British motorist abroad is that of remembering to Keep To The Right Of The Road in France and other countries where this whimsical rule obtains. But this, like parachuting, tracheotomy and playing the Nubian nose-flute, is simply a matter of practice. During his first day or so on foreign soil the beginner may suffer a few

The "Plein Air" Coupe

*Futile Attempt to Get Used to Driving on the Right Hand
Side of the Road*

minor collisions, which will teach him how like verbal
knitting French can be when uttered by incensed French
persons; but he will soon conquer his Leftist tendencies
and adhere to the Right as rigidly as any Rear-Admiral
(retd.).

Experience, indeed, is the only safe guide in this
matter. Experiments with mirrors, such as that suggested
in the accompanying sketch, are inadvisable. In that
position no motorist looks his best, while the prolonged
contemplation of his own face does no man any good.

Motorists of modest means (well, aren't we all?)
are prone to imagine that the cost of foreign touring
is so high as to be almost out of reach. Well, so it can
be, of course, for those who like that sort of thing—
those who stop only at the best hotels, eat only caviare
and ortolans, and wear real silk next to their skin. But
otherwise, apart from the essential outlay on petrol,
oil, amusing postcards and that macabre fluid which

108

is the foreigner's conception of beer, it need cost no more and no less than the tourist chooses to cough up.

If the motorist is fairly tough, the weather fairly good and his car fairly adaptable, he need not stop at hotels much; and if he can buy, borrow, charter or purloin a caravan, he need not stop at them at all. In this connection, I would draw the attention of all to Mr. Heath Robinson's design for a compact family caravan, a blue-print of which is appended overleaf.

In this vehicle, which was evolved by Mr. Heath Robinson for a tour of the Dolomites (after he had been finally convinced that Dolomites are not, as he had always supposed, little greyish insects that creep out of woodwork in damp weather), a small family can live happily for several weeks and in several places.

As the drawing shows, the He-Ro-Van is shapely, weatherproof, and equipped with every modern convenience except a service lift, a television-set and

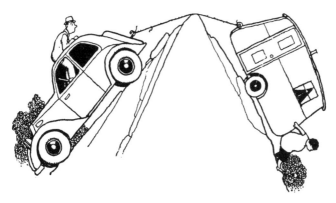

An Alpine Impasse

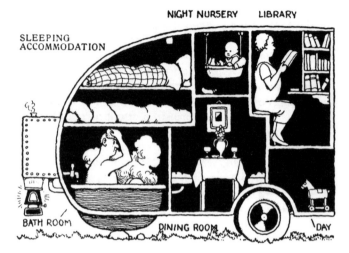

SLEEPING ACCOMMODATION

NIGHT NURSERY   LIBRARY

BATH ROOM   DINING ROOM   DAY

Interior of

an umbrella-stand; but these refinements can be added at a small extra cost. The combined library-and-day-nursery is a notably happy thought, as it enables the Little Woman (or the Big one, as in the illustration) to keep (a) abreast of current trends in Literature and (b) an eye on Junior. The occupant of the bath, incidentally, is a Mr. P.W. Mitten-Whale-bone, a retired dealer in second-hand coffins, who happened to be passing at the time and smilingly consented to pose for the picture; not that it matters really.

Although Mr. Heath Robinson ("Towser" to me) and I ("Stinker" to him) naturally regard this as the best all-round, all-purposes, all-British, all-plywood caravan obtainable, there are as many other types on the market as there are pips in a grapefruit.

the Family Caravan

The would-be tourist has only to seek until he finds one that wins his heart and imposes no intolerable strain upon his pocket, and then attach his car to it and get going.

It is essential, by the way, that the caravan be *firmly* attached to the car by a proper gadget, and not merely hitched to it with a bit of string. No conscientious driver can simultaneously look ahead and astern, and there is nothing more disconcerting to a trans-Continental tourist than the discovery, on his arrival at Cannes, that his caravan, containing all his beer, his personal effects, his spare socks and his loved ones, has come unstuck on the outskirts of Paris.

Just one more point in this connection, if everybody can stand it. As sudden inrushes of water detract from

The Anti-Wet Caravan

the comfort of caravans, it is a good plan, when touring in flooded areas or during a typical English summer, to have the vehicle fitted with four stout telescopic legs, worked from indoors by small hand-winches. By this means the caravan can be raised bodily above high-water mark, if need be, and kept there until the floods subside, its inmates beguiling the hours with rod and line meanwhile.

So much for the caravan-de-luxe, or home-on-wheels-from-home. Not everybody, unfortunately, can

The Trailerette,

afford one of these super-models; but with a little forethought, ingenuity and a few spare quid, almost anybody can go caravanning in a modest way.

For touring rainless regions, for example—such as Death Valley (Ariz.), the Desert of Gobi and the drier bits of Australia—a home-made trailerette, as here depicted, will be found as useful as it is inexpensive. Constructed of such humble materials as a superannuated bicycle, a disused perambulator and a barn door borrowed from a kindly neighbour, it costs but a few shillings, ex works, and enables a small party to enjoy the benefits of fresh air, regular meals and perpetual motion without any expenditure of energy.

It is true that the members of the said party will probably get shied at more than once by nervous horses and stared at a good deal by boorish passers-by, but this will encourage them to shave regularly,

For Touring Deserts

remember their table-manners and cultivate that air of aloof detachment which is so helpful in public life.

For Continental touring on a modest income, the Heath Robinson "In-A-Trice Karbedde" is strongly recommended. This is simply an expanding bed (as used in time of war by the lesser members of Divisional Staffs) screwed to the rear of the car and fitted with a tasteful mahogany doorknob whereby it can be fully extended in no time when Night casts her sable mantle o'er the sylvan scene and a little healing shut-eye seems indicated. Thanks to the "Karbedde", the touring motorist and his *alter ego*, the motoring tourist, can curl up with a tired sigh by the roadside anywhere between Boulogne and Bordighera and dream the long hours away in perfect comfort at a total cost of less than one (1) *centime*.

Although the Continental landowner is not quite so determined to keep himself to himself, his property inviolate and strangers at a distance as is his British counterpart, the Briton abroad should always use a little sense—and even more, if he has any—when choosing a camping-site. To bed down for the night

The "In-a-Trice Karbedde"

For Touring Mountainous Districts

in the drive of somebody else's *chateau*, in the middle of a *Route Nationale* or in the *Grande Place* of a country town on the eve of a market-day is to invite a good deal of assorted trouble. It is widely believed abroad that most of the English are slightly weak in the head; nor, having regard to our licensing regulations, our betting-laws and our unflinching devotion to boiled cabbage, is this surprising. Nevertheless, there are certain things that not even an Englishman can do and get away with on a plea of insanity.

In very mountainous districts, where Alps are three a penny and the skyline resembles a magnified oleograph of an ill-made set of false teeth; the roads often go up and down so drastically as to induce vertigo in nervous motorists. Thanks to Mr. Heath Robinson, however—

who sat up all night over it, with a wet towel round his feet and his head in a mustard bath—this difficulty is now overcome. By fixing telescopic, self-operating springs between his wheels and his chassis—quite an easy feat for the mechanically minded—the motorist can keep his car at all times on so even a keel that the back seat passengers will be uncertain whether they are coming, going, flying or whizzing up and down in a lift. This will cause much amusement, and a good time will be had by all.

Just one more suggestion, and then we can all pop out for a quick one. Even foreign scenery (which differs from our home-grown variety in being knobbier, flatter or just bigger, as a rule) tends to pall in time, and towards the end of a long tour the motorist is liable to yearn for something to take his mind off it. As any doctor will attest, the best cure for this type of *ennui* is a brisk game of snooker, under Jockey Club rules and with strangleholds barred. Motorists who are easily bored, therefore, are advised to include a small legless billiards-table in their kit before they cross the Channel. When not required for play, the table can be borne like a shield at the back of the car as a protection against stray bullets, meteorites and turnips flung from ambush, while the cues can be used as emergency alpenstocks and the balls as things to throw at bandits.

If there are any questions about any other aspect of motoring abroad that anybody would like to ask, will they kindly record them in block letters on a stamped postcard and address it to the Foreign Office (Fatuous Query Dept.)? To apply to Mr. Heath Robinson and/or myself would be sheer waste of a stamp, partly because we shall probably be out on our tandem-cycle, and partly because (we feel) we have dealt with the subject as exhaustively as any subject can be dealt with on a damp afternoon by two elderly gentlemen with rheumatism.

In other words, we have nothing more to say, except possibly: "Good night, everybody (and that includes you, madam, with the string-bag and the strabismus)! Good night!"

Snooker

Improved Road Manners

TAILPIECE

Finis coronat opus. Although Mr. Heath Robinson and I are not agreed as to the meaning of this phrase—he insisting that it is a *quinquecento* Italian oath, and I maintaining that it is part of an old Roman recipe for fishcakes—we feel somehow that it is a fitting observation with which to bring these proceedings to a close. (And about time, too, as the stout gentleman in Row B so justly remarks.)

As we pointed out elsewhere, this modest but quite attractive little book is not intended for experienced motorists or for those passionate mechanical experts who rank almost as honorary spanners. It is designed to assist, soothe and instruct the motorist-in-embryo who longs to join the procession on the Kingston By-Pass but is uncertain how to set about it. If, in addition, it cures him of insomnia, there will be no extra charge.

Our most fervent admirer (a Mr. Jno. Woonsocket, of Peebles, who had to leave England in a hurry and a false moustache last April, to our regret) would not claim that we have said *everything* that can be said about

118

Improved Road Manners

motoring, its cause, prevention and cure. After all, as any pedestrian will agree, there are certain things that cannot decently be said in print, or when there are ladies present. Still, we do feel that we have done rather more than our bit—inasmuch as nobody asked us to do anything—to make this great Empire even more motor-minded than it is at present, and to enable Britain's motor-manufacturers to enjoy an occasional kipper with their tea during the coming year.

If those motor manufacturers, by the way, consider our efforts on their behalf deserving of some slight acknowledgment, such as a couple of (tax-free)

Uncertain How To Set About It

limousines or two bunches of artificial wall-flowers, we would just like to say that we rather feel that way about it, too. And if, as a result of our labours in the cause of Bigger and Better Motoring, a nation-wide improvement in road-manners generally is not very shortly apparent, we shall both be profoundly grieved, but not—let's face it—intensely surprised.

The End